And the Birds are Singing

Rebecca Stallard

Prep and Partners Publishing
Kansas City, Missouri

Prep and Partners Publishing
Kansas City, Missouri

Copyright, 2008
Rebecca Stallard
All rights reserved

Manufactured in the United States of America

United States Copyright Office
Rebecca Stallard

And
the
Birds
are
Singing

ISBN
978-0-615-25304-6

Edited by Brenda Conley

A special thanks to
Valorie Stokes
&
Heidi Mick

The publication of this book is
dedicated to four generations
of my family, who, through
their heartache and
suffering, were led to help
future generations.

Cover Photo
The Bird Family
1961
&
Esther and Wesley

Technical Support
and cover design
Ralph Acosta

www.rebeccastallard.com

Table of Contents

Esther	1
1898 – Bird Makes Turkey	2
Etta Bird	3
1904	4
Bird Seed	5
Grandmother Kindle	6
1918	8
1924	9
Ten in the 20's, 30's & 40's	10
The Great Depression	12
Learning to Fly	13
1943 – Falling from the Nest	14
Nest Eggs	15
The Wings of a Dove	16
About – Mrs. Jewell	17
Little Bohemian Sparrow Part I	18
Little Bohemian Sparrow Part II	19
Order in the Nest	20
Kitty	21
Bird Banter	22
Empty Pockets	24
Bird Watching	25
Homing Pigeon	26
The Wise, Young Owl	27
Fly Away Little Birdie, Part I	28
Upon Sunset	29
Birds of Kansas	30
Breakfast is for the Birds	31
The Early Birds Eat the Dust	32
A Bird in the Hand is Better	34
Five Steps on Turning Four	35
Two Birds with One Stone	36
Hummingbirds	37
Bird Menagerie	38
Dreams to Fly	39

Some Birds Fly – Some Swim – Some Run	40
Fowl Play	41
Passing the Branch	42
Myna Bird	44
Another Type of Bird	45
About Tommy – On Soaring High	46
Broken Wing	47
CAW	48
The Clever Bird	49
The Bird with a Bill	50
Fly Away Little Birdie, Part II	51
High Pockets	52
Phil	53
Blue Jays	54
Levi's Lament	55
Mocking Birds	56
The Swan in a Uniform	58
Two Birds Flying in Circles	59
Slow Poke	60
John	61
Married to a Jail Bird	62
About – The 4th of July	63
I Love to Hear the Birds when they Sing	64
Parakeets and Cockatiels … Part I	65
When the Score was Tied at Twenty	66
Parakeets and Cockatiels … Part II	67
Leaving the Nest	68
Night Owl	69
I Know you're Talking, but…	70
Gerald meets a Cardinal …	72
Plumage	73
Love Birds	74
Ann Mary – the Blue-Eyed Stork	76
Tommy	77
About Darlene – Moving to Colorado	78
About Kenny – Becoming a Kingbird	79

Bill, Bill from Over the Hill, …	80
The Sea Gull	81
Birds of Paradise, Part I	82
No More the Baby Bird	83
Setting Wings to Soar	84
About Virginia	85
A New Song	86
Flying South	87
Searching for Shelter	88
Bird on a Wire	89
William Orton	90
Western Union	91
Birds of Passage	92
Birding	93
Funny	94
Little Bohemian Pig	95
Not all Birds can Fly…	96
An Old Bird Learns a New Trick	97
When he was Four and Twenty	98
About – Virginia's Missing Feathers	99
Birds of a Feather	100
About – The Words Virginia Spoke…	101
In the Stillness of the Midnight	102
Published	103
Bird Brain	104
Pretty Bird	105
About Darlene – Leaving Colorado	106
DNA	107
Bird in a Box	108
The Bird Cage	109
Parakeets and Cockatiels … Part III	110
A Little Bird Once Told Me	111
Without Words, Part I	112
Without Words, Part II	113
Without Words, Part III	114
Cancer	115

A Whisper of the Wind	116
About – How I Reacted …	118
A Tough Old Bird	120
About – The 1977 4th of July Reunion	121
As the Wind Blows	122
About – My Thirteen-Year-Old Granddaughter	123
Mary Ann and Me	124
About – The Birthday Party	126
About – Time	128
Birds of Paradise, Part II	129
The Flight Continues, Part I, II, III, IV & V	130
The Flight Continues, Part VI	131
Posthumous Fame	132
Let's Put 'it' to Rest	133
Air Above Wings	134

Esther

To know the reason
I reacted as I did
on that particular day,
you would have to
know
a few things about
my life.

You would have to
know my father …

the tragedy about
my mother,

and
you would
definitely
have to know
about the lives
of my children.

And then,
just maybe,
you would
understand
why…

Why
I reacted as
I did
on
that
particular day.

— 1898 —
Bird Makes Turkey

My father's name was
Levi Leonard Bird.

In 1898,
Levi purchased a
fine new buggy.

The townsfolk
wondered why
he drove it through
all that ice and snow
on Thanksgiving Day
to have dinner with
his lady-friend, Etta.

But then they understood,
as apparently,
there was
more 'Trotting' going on …
than
with the turkey.

After they ate
Thanksgiving Dinner,
Levi and Etta
exchanged
their marriage vows.

Etta Bird

My father, Levi, and my
mother, Etta, were farmers.

As raising things is the
proper task for farmers,
Levi and Etta took on to raising
a little girl.

Etta gave birth to my older
sister, Lola Mae Bird, on
a Sunday… they skipped
church that day.

My parents were happier than
they ever imagined possible.

Two years later, another
crop was harvested.

I was brought into the world.
My name is Esther Mina Bird.

… But I never got to know
my mother.

1904

By knowing the story of Levi Leonard Bird and how
Important his wife, Etta, was to him, you would be
Reminded of true love. And by knowing that Etta
Died at twenty-eight years of age, you would
Sadly be reminded

Of how suffering will occasionally
Fall into someone's life. But you should

Always be reminded that the deepest of all sorrow will

Fade over time. … My mother,
Etta, left behind two beautiful-baby girls
And my father, Levi, was okay. — We reminded him
To smile. And Levi had a different kind of help as well.
His mother would visit and bring with her a sense of humor.
Each evening, she would sit on the front porch,
Rock in her chair, tell stories, and smoke her pipe.

Bird Seed

My father, Levi, loved his beer.

He loved it even more after the
death of my mother; but he never
over-indulged, because he had
me and my older sister to raise.

My father, Levi, had an auction
and sold his farm.

He bought a Blacksmith shop

And worked…

…and worked

…and worked.

Grandmother Kindle

Levi moved his mother in
to raise and nurture us girls;
and Levi hired a woman
to help with daily chores.

The woman moved about the house,
to tend to daily needs;
but Levi's mother, with watchful eye,
warned Levi to take heed.

"That woman that cleans around the house
is looking for a man.
She struts about with tempting ways
doing everything she can,
to make you look and try to hook
before she reels you in.
I warn you son, to rid her now,
Before she causes sin."

"Oh, mother, don't be silly,
I think you're being mean;
the woman is merely doing her job,
she's here to cook and clean."

But Levi, taking notice,
Noticed shape and noticed form;
And within his soul, within his flesh,
began a raging storm.

He smiled upon the woman,
she smiled upon him too.
Inside his heart he fell in love,
but didn't know what to do.

Levi told his mother,
"I soon again shall marry."
But mother Kindle, with stern, full-force, then
acted kind of scary!

"I forbid you, Son, to take a wife.
The girls need YOU and ME!
That other woman in our life,
you tell her she is free.
For I will cook the food,
raise the girls and do the cleaning,
we need no others in our life
to give it love and meaning."

So… Levi obeyed his mother,
with heavy heart and much regret.
He bid farewell unto the woman,
and said, "I will never forget."

Then Levi and his mother
raised us girls as best they could—
they gave us hope—gave us love;
they gave us all that parents should.

1918

Grandmother Kindle?

    Yes, Esther.

What can you tell me about my mother?

    She was very pretty, Esther.

What else?

    She was a good cook and a wonderful mother.

What else?

    Child, I'm tired; now run along and do your chores.

Please, Grandmother Kindle. Please tell me.

    (Sigh!) Your father loved her very much.

And she loved him, too?

    More than life itself, Esther. More than life itself. I'm tired, now, child. Please, just run along.

Good-bye Grandmother, Kindle.

    Good-bye my darling, Esther. Good-bye.

1924

Every time I saw him, I
Smiled. — As
Time gave way to love,
He asked for my hand.
Evening fell to dawn, and
Rain gave way to a sun-lit morning.

~

Working the land on our farm, we
Ever-so-happily, began a new life.
Seeking only one another, we
Lived to honor our love. — We
Endured each day,
Yielding to trust and duty.

Ten in the 20's 30's & 40's

One, two, three,
four and five.
One-at-a-time,
the kids arrive.

Six, seven, eight,
nine and ten.
It's different now
than it was back then.

So many children!
Who could keep track
Of all of those kids
playing out back?

Darlene, Virginia,
Helen and Ken,
That's only four,
there should be ten.

Lorraine, Gerald,
Jean and Mary,
And after Donald,
along came Gerry.

So many kids
to feed and bathe,
So many kids
to make behave.

Then Grandpa Bird
gave them all nick-names.

What was he thinking?
Is he to blame
For all the confusion
in the house of ten,
which now was twenty,
all kin to Ken;

I mean,
John & Slow Poke
&
High-Pockets & Funny…
&
Little-Bohemian Pig
&
Tippy, Tippy Tom-boy
&
AAAAAHHHHhhhhhh!!!!

So many children.
Who could keep track
Of all those kids
playing out back?
Who could see the difference
in every face?
Who could give love
with gentle embrace?

The answer to the question
remains with another.

I could! — Because
I was their mother.

The Great Depression

When pride fell, passion ceased.
Empty hands and a vacant heart, caused
Solace to depart. — We
Lost our farm…and more.
Even Wesley's 1926 Model-T was
Yielded—piece by piece for food.

~

Everything was moved to Levi's. —
Silence occupied days and
Tolerance from Wesley was nil. But
Heaven disclosed deliverance, and
Each day my children
Responded to a sense of duty.

Learning to Fly

After her first day of Kindergarten,
Darlene came home and declared,
"Grandpa Bird and Mommy...
I don't need to go back to school
because everything they taught me
today, I already know."

~

That same day, after lunch, Levi
returned to work at the Blacksmith
shop, and I noticed that little Kenny
had disappeared. I was frantic, not
knowing where my toddler was.

Darlene and Virginia helped me in
my desperate search.

Then, I found him ... he was down at the
Blacksmith shop playing with some of
the shop-tools and helping his grandfather.

Each of my children loved spending
time with their grandfather. And
my father, loved spending time with
them.

— 1943 —
Falling from the Nest

Rock of Ages, cleft for me,
Is the song we sang that morning. I gave birth to another
Child on Sunday, May 16th. But
Heaven called the child home on Monday, May 17th.
All my children were sad. Wesley and I, especially hurt.
Richard. Little baby, Richard. Our hearts are broken,
Desiring to know who you would have been.

Nest Eggs

President Roosevelt said that
many jobs will soon be created.
Hopefully, my husband, Wesley,
will be able to find
full-time employment.

Our country is in the middle
of a war. They are spending
lots and lots of money
to send our men
to fight.

But here,
right in the middle of our country,
we don't see much of a war,
we only know
there is no money to spend.

My sister, Lola Mae, moved
to California. She said she
wanted to become one of those
"Rosie the Riveter" girls and
work on the Liberator airplanes.

She said if we came to California
We could find work. But I can't.
I cannot take my children away
from my father.

They have become his life.

The Wings of a Dove

Levi worked at his Blacksmith shop from 6:00 a.m. to 6:00 p.m., seven days a week; (with an hour lunch).

However, on Sunday morning during the church service, some of the townsfolk complained that too much noise came from his shop.

… But instead of going to my father, the town council held a special meeting, after which, the mayor banned Levi from working on Sunday.

Levi unwillingly agreed and then did what any dedicated, hard-working, blacksmith would do…
just past midnight on Sunday,
when Monday "technically" arrived,
he began work — banging metal,
hammering plow blades, making horseshoes, etc.

Not long after, the townsfolk said that he may resume working on Sunday… and Levi, being the gentleman that he was, waited until noon, after Sunday services were concluded, before opening up his shop.

About —
Mrs. Jewell

One of the most respected ladies of the town, Mrs. Jewell, would often comment to other folks. She would say, "Esther's children may not always have socks to wear, or warm coats in the winter, but I have never seen a happier or friendlier bunch of kids. Esther's children have always impressed me."

... I wish Wesley could find work.

Little Bohemian Sparrows
Part I

My father, Levi,
a.k.a. Grandpa Bird,
often told his grandchildren
how their ancestors
came from the far-away-land
of artists, musicians, actors and poets.

He said it was traditional for everyone to
have a given name, as well as a pretend one.

Levi gave the name of "Slow-poke"
to his granddaughter, Helen; teasing her
because she was a hard worker.

To his granddaughter, Virginia, Levi gave
The name of her current boyfriend. Phil.

Mary Ann was called, "Ann Mary".

Donald was called, "Bill, Bill from over the hill,
never worked and never will." He too,
was a hard worker.

Levi smiled at his grandchildren as he
rocked in his rocker and smoked his pipe.
He was incredibly proud of them all.

Little Bohemian Sparrows
Part II

Darlene was the oldest grandchild
of Levi. Darlene's clothes
were often too small,
so she was known as, "High-Pockets".

Jean was the youngest,
her clothes were often worn out.
She was called, "Little Bohemian Pig".

Geraldine didn't like the name, Geraldine,
So she named herself, Gerry; but Grandpa Bird
named her, "Funny".

He called Ken, John; and Lorraine,
(who pitched on the boys baseball team)
He called, "Tippy-tippy-tom-boy,"
and later, Tommy.

Gerald was known as the Sea Gull.

Levi smiled at his grandchildren as he
rocked in his rocker and smoked his pipe.
He was incredibly proud of
all of his little Bohemian sparrows.

Order in the Nest

Darlene	- High Pockets
Virginia	- Phil
Helen	- Slow Poke
Kenny	- John
Mary Ann	- Ann Mary
Lorraine	- Tommy
Donald	- Bill, Bill from over the Hill
Gerald	- The Sea Gull
Geraldine	- Funny (Gerry)
Richard	-
Jean	- Little Bohemian Pig

Kitty

I love playing the card game, Pinochle.
I especially like playing 'three-handed,'
because if you get the bid, you get the
extra cards from the kitty.

Whenever I say, 'I just love having the
kitty,' little Mary Ann always says,
"Meow."

Bird Banter

"Grandpa Bird?"

"Yes, Virginia."

"Why do you own a Blacksmith Shop?"

"Hmmm. Well, let's see. When my father died,
my mother married George Kindle, and he's the one
who taught me the trade. However, I was a farmer.
But when my wife died, I sold the farm
and built my own Blacksmith shop."

"Oh. Well, why didn't you want to get
married again after your wife died?"

"Virginia, it's not that I didn't want to,
my wife's two sisters said they would
take away Esther and your Aunt Lola if
I did. So my mother came to live with
me and made sure that I didn't get
married again."

"Was that your saddest year … When your
wife died?"

"Yes, Virginia, it was; that and 1894."

"What happened in 1894?"

"My, you are just full of questions this evening."

"Tell me what happened, Grandpa. Please."

"Well, in April of 1894, one of my stables burned to the ground. My friend John Dearborn risked his life to save my horse. Then in November of that same year, someone broke a window in my stepfather's Blacksmith Shop and they thieved some of our tools."

"What else happened, Grandpa?"

"It's my turn to ask you a question, now, Virginia. Are you merely asking me questions so you don't have to go to bed?"

"Yes, Sir."

"Goodnight, Virginia."

"Goodnight, Grandpa."

Empty Pockets

"Esther!"

"Yes. What is it now, Wesley?"

"I want all those damn kids to be quiet. I'm Trying to take a nap."

"Yes, dear."

"Mommy?"

"Yes, Darlene."

"Why is Daddy always mad?"

"I don't know, Darlene."

"Is it because he has to work for the butcher and all he gets to bring home are the left-over parts... like the brains and stuff?"

"It could be, Darlene."

"Well, Helen says they're not so bad if you fry them in a skillet and douse them with mustard."

"Let me put it to you this way, Darlene. They're not so bad if you're hungry and that's all you've got to eat."

Bird Watching

"MOMMY!"

        "Virginia, keep your voice down,
you'll wake your father."

"But where is Tommy? She's supposed
to help me with the dishes. Gerry, have
you seen Tommy?"

        "Yes."

"Well, where did she go?"

        "Uh...
        Uh... well... she snuck
         out the bedroom window
        to go and play baseball."

"MOMMY!"

        "Virginia, keep your voice down,
you'll wake your father."

Homing Pigeon

Wesley finally found full-time employment,
working out-of-state for the railroad near the
Navajo reservation.
For a short time, he forgot about the pain of
being impoverished.

Wesley found new friends in his co-workers.
They taught him the Navajo language.
For a short time, he forgot that he could also
speak English, German & Czech.

Wesley had icy-blue eyes and blonde hair.
His Navajo co-workers nicknamed him,
"Whitey."
For a short time, he forgot that his name
was really, Wesley.

Wesley became the foreman. He was known
as the leader, and the 200 men below him,
were known as "The Extra-gang".

Wesley knew that working sun-up to sun-down,
was the only way to make a decent living.
For a short time, he forgot that his men needed to rest.

So on occasion, Wesley drank, played cards, and
had a good time with his new-found friends.

And for the longest time, he forgot that he had a
wife and ten children back at home.

The Wise, Young Owl

My father, Levi, was fond of chocolate. He often treated his grandchildren to the sweetness of Hershey's chocolate candy bars.

Every evening, when he came home from work, my father hung up his coat on the coat rack, then went upstairs.

Tonight, however, he went upstairs first; then came down and hung up his coat on the coat rack.

Ken noticed his grandfather's unusual routine and became suspicious. He went upstairs to investigate. Ken smiled when he discovered his grandfather's plan… A Hershey's candy-bar box, filled with corn-cobs.

Ken had a secret-family meeting with his siblings. They pooled their money and bought enough candy bars to replace the corn-cobs.

On April 1st, my father was grinning from ear to ear as he came downstairs, carrying a box, marked "Hershey's Chocolate Candy Bars."

"Gather round," he said. "I have a special surprise," and he handed the box to his grandchildren.

Ken smiled, knowing who was indeed the true April fool.

My father was dumbfounded as he watched his grand-children laughing and enjoying themselves as they devoured the Hershey's chocolate candy bars.

Fly Away Little Birdie
Part I

"Helen?"

        "Yes, Mother."

"Would you like to go live
with Mrs. Jewell for the winter
and work for her?"

        "Mommy, she's so big,
        she can't even reach down
        to button her own shoes."

"That's why she needs help, Helen.
Keep in mind all of the nice things
she's done for our family.
Remember, it's only until spring."

        "Okay, I guess I will. I'll
        go."

Upon Sunset

I, Esther, missed Wesley.

Wesley, worked on the railroad.
I stayed at home with the children.
The children, played and worked.

"When will daddy be home?" asked
the children.
"Soon," I said.

I, Esther, missed Wesley.

I, Esther, rode on a train with baby, Jean; headed
for a surprise visit to see Wesley.
"That's a mighty cute baby you've got there,"
said the conductor.
"Thank you," I said.

I, Esther, at the hotel near the railroad.

I inquired upon the clerk, "In which room
is Wesley staying, please?"
The clerk, smiled. "You mean, Whitey? ...
Well, he and his wife are over in
room twelve. Say, that's a mighty cute baby
you've got there!"
"Thank you," I said.

I, Esther, with baby Jean
on a train headed home.

I, Esther, never missed
Wesley again.

Birds of Kansas

The birds flew round
And made the sound
Of music that would soon abound.
…They sang to hearts content.

Their songs gave heir
To laughter fair
And was the answer to their prayer.
…They lived as life was meant.

~

Ken shined shoes outside the bakery and
was paid a loaf of bread.
He delivered milk for the milk man and
was paid a quart of milk.

Helen worked for peanuts, literally.
After working odd jobs for Mrs. Jewell,
Helen used some of her nickels to buy
peanut clusters to share with her siblings.

Darlene and Virginia became waitresses
at the local café.
Their wages helped to feed the family.

Some might say that life was hard for
my children. But my children didn't
know any different.

They took life as it came, and they
always, and I mean always, smiled at
those who passed their way.

Breakfast is for the Birds

Each and every morning, just before the break of dawn, I rose from a restful slumber to prepare breakfast for my children. Usually, I could only afford eggs; but on rare occasions, when Wesley sent money home from the railroad, I would cook a special made-to-order breakfast for each and every one of my children.

For Darlene and Virginia, I usually made their favorite buttermilk-pancakes. For Ken, Don and Gerald, it was bacon, eggs and hash-brown potatoes. Helen required only a simple cup of coffee. For Mary Ann and Tommy, it was French toast and oatmeal — for Gerry, cinnamon toast, served with a chilled glass of carefully-blended chocolate-milk — and for Jean, toast, layered with old-fashioned, canned-strawberry jam.

My children have always valued my kindness, even on the days that breakfast is limited; and that is why they rise from a restful slumber each and every morning just before the break of dawn ... to deliver newspapers before attending school and working their afternoon and evening jobs.

The Early Birds Eat the Dust

"Hey, Gerry!"

    "What do you want, Tommy?"

. . . .
swinging around a rope she had found
. . . .

"Let's pretend to be a snake."

    "How?"

"Put this around your waist."

    "Okay."

"Now, let's start running up the road, I'll be on the left side and you be on the right. When you see me cross over to the right side, you cross over to the left. Then when I cross to the left, you cross to the right. The rope should look just like a snake that is slithering up the road. 'On your mark, get set, go!'"

~~~~~~~~~~~~~~~~~~~~~~~~~~~~~~~~~~~~

    "It's working. it does look like a snake."

. . . .
oblivious to the car, coming from afar
. . . .

    . . . .
    Rope tangled & mangled; girls spinning around
    The only words that they could sound
    . . . .

"Help!"

       "Help!"

"Somebody Help!"

       "Help us!"

. . . .
Running; Stunning; fast and brave.
Brother, Kenny, there to save
. . . .

       "Mr. Roper! Stop the Car.
       Please, Mr. Roper. My sisters."

. . . .
Dresses, torn; images, worn
. . . .

       "Are you okay, Tommy?"

"I think so; but my knees got all
skinned up and my chin got cut."

       "Gerry. Are you okay?"

       "All I know is that Tommy wanted to
       Play like a snake.
       Cars shouldn't be in the habit of
       Running over snakes.
       (tears)
       And my dress got all torn in the wheel.
       Mommy is going to be mad."

       "Mother will not be mad, Gerry. She
       will just make you take a bath."

A Bird in the Hand is Better

Hey there, Funny.

    Hi, Grandpa.

What cha doing? I caught ya cheatin' didn't I?

    I'm not cheating, Grandpa. I'm just playing cards.

Why don't you play Solitaire?

    That's what I'm playing!

Well, then, put the three up there on the top stack.

    Oh. Thank you, Grandpa. I didn't see that.

Now, move the Queen over to the King and turn over that card. Now you can put the ten over on the Jack, put the King in the empty space and turn over th... What? ... Why are you giving Grandpa that dirty look?

    It's not a dirty look, Grandpa. I already
    know how to play.

Well, if you don't need your old grandpa, I guess I'll just... uh... go ... and ... uh ...

    Grandpa? ... Grandpa!

Uh ... oh, what cha need, Funny?

    Thanks for helping me play cards.

You're welcome, Gerry. You are welcome.

Five Steps on Turning Four

Step One:
Gerald leaves the parlor and closes the door. Gerald enters the kitchen and fills a glass with water. Gerald re-enters the parlor.

Step Two:
Gerald leaves the parlor and closes the door. Gerald enters the kitchen and fills a glass with water. Gerald re-enters the parlor.

Step Three:
Repeat steps one and two. Add Ken taking notice.

Step Four:
Ken enters the parlor; he yells, "Fire! The parlor curtains are on fire!"

Step Five
Speaking to my son. "Gerald, when you have a birthday, remember, it's Mommy's job to light the candles on your cake."

Two Birds with One Stone

Tommy?

       Yes, Jean.

Why did Grandpa Bird name you Tommy, when you're a girl?

       Because my real name is Lorraine Frances;
       and everybody kept saying "Lorraine
       Frances wets her pantses." Plus, I'm kind
       of a Tom-boy.

Oh. Well, why did he name me Little Bohemian Pig?

       (smile)
       Because you try to keep up with nine
       older brothers and sisters. And Daddy's
       family came from Bohemia.

Does that mean I'll be a poet and a singer?

       More than likely, Jean. More than likely.

Hummingbirds

Gerry could hover over a situation and
rapidly scold whomever she felt wasn't
holding up their end of responsibility.

--Pick up your clothes.
--You need to wash your own dishes.
--Why haven't you collected the chicken
    eggs?
--You need to weed the garden.
--Whose turn is it to dust?
--Don't drink that beer, it stinks!

Jean and Helen could always calm their
sister by humming a little tune.
One of their favorites was, "This Ole House",
sung by Rosemary Clooney.

Jean would hum a few notes to herself.
Helen would give Jean a little wink, and
join in on the humming.

Soon after, Jean and Helen would softly
echo aloud the lyrics; and before long, the
trio was in tune and Gerry was calm.

Bird Menagerie

Gooch Red-Circle-Round-Up-Day was a Christmas tradition in town.

Perhaps it became a tradition because it was a convention of the Christmas spirit.

Nonetheless, Gooch Red – Circle – Round - Up - Day gave many families the opportunity to fetch a hearty Christmas dinner.

For the festivities, donations were made by many of the local businesses. — But the most important donations of the day had to be caught.

The best part of Gooch Red-Circle-Round-Up-Day was the round-up itself.

A small menagerie of turkeys, hens, ducks, one goose and several white rabbits were turned loose in the church-yard arena; and after the games began, the children of the town played the oldest known-form of Duck-Duck-Goose.

The birds and rabbits squawked and squawked as they ran in circles. The children laughed and laughed as they ran and chased their prey.

The prize caught, was the prize kept.

This year, three of the turkeys went to the Winklepleck's and the Wagoners. Little Rodney VanKirk caught the goose. Donald and Lorraine caught two of the hens and Kenny caught one of the white rabbits.

My father, Levi, and I were as proud as punch.

Christmas dinner would be plentiful this year, all because of Gooch Red-Circle-Round-Up-Day.

Dreams to Fly

Tommy?

    Yes, Helen.

What are your dreams?

    I want to play baseball.

Other than that?

    I don't know. I guess travel.

Me too.

    Where are you going to go?

Anywhere. Everywhere. Away from this tiny town. I want to see the world.

    Me too.

Let's make a pact.

    Okay.

Let's save our money, buy a car, never get married, and travel where ever we want to go.

    That is a deal!

Tommy?

    Yes, Helen.

Promise?

    I promise.

Some Birds Fly — Some Swim — Some Run

Hey, John? ...   ... John! ...   ... Kenneth.

Right here, Grandpa, Bird.

How old are you now, son?

I'm thirteen.

How would you like a job?

I have a job, Sir. Several, in fact.

How about a job that pays in beer?

Even better.

I'll tell you what I need... I used to travel to Kansas City about twice a year and bring back beer in nail kegs. Now that prohibition is over, I don't have to sneak around so much, but ... I'm getting along in years ... and well, I need a man ... a good man ... to be my beer runner. You in?

Yes, Sir!

Good. Just so you know — I never drink beer on Sunday...unless it's my birthday. And, Ken?

Yes, Sir?

Never feel sorry for yourself... and never be a cheater.

Yes, Sir, Grandpa Bird. And thank you.

You're welcome, Kenneth.

Fowl Play

I smelled smoke just about the time that
Donald came barreling into the house.
"Mom. The side porch is on fire.
I'm sorry. I'm so sorry.
I promise
I will never play with matches again.
… Ever."

I quenched the flames with several
buckets of water just about the time
that Wesley came barreling out of the house.
"Esther. Where is that boy?
He's going to be sorry.
I swear on my life
that his butt will be on fire,
… Forever!"

Passing the Branch

Hey, Ken?

>What do you want, Darlene?

Virginia and I want to sell the paper route. You interested?

>How much will I make?

About $8.00 a month.

>I'll take it.

~

>Hey, Helen?

What do you want, Ken?

I get paid $2.00 a week for my paper route. If you'd like a job, I'll split the money with you.

>What about a bicycle, won't I need a bike?

>>You'll have to work out a deal with Bill Trulisky; you in?

>Yeah, I'm in.

~

>Hey, Gerry.

>>What do you want, Helen?

I want to sell you the paper route.

>How much for the bike?

Ten.

> That bike's not worth ten dollars. There's no bar grips, no chain guard, the pedals are broken and it needs new tires. How about six?

Deal.

~

> Mommy?

>> Yes, Geraldine.

> Sometimes there's a bum in the train depot when I pick up the papers; and…well, bums scare me.

>> Why don't you ask one of your brothers or sisters to help you?"

> Will I have to share the money?"

>> Yes. You'll have to share the money.

~

> Hey, Jean?

What do you want, Gerry?

> You and Gerald want to help me with the paper route? I'll pay you.

Yes.

> Okay, but remember, for some of the subscribers you have to place their paper under a brick on the back porch; and for others, right beside the front door.

How will I know which customer's get what?

> You will just have to learn.

Myna Bird

Mommy?

        Yes, Mary Ann?

Is that one kind of Bird spelled,
M – Y – N – A, and pronounced "mean-a" bird?
And your name spelled,
M – I – N – A, and pronounced "mine-a" Bird?

        Yes, Mary Ann.

Where did that name come from?

        My mother. Before she married, her name
        was Ester Mina Hogue; only people called
        her Etta.

Oh. … Well, I'm sorry you never knew her… your mother.

        I am, too, Mary Ann. But in some way, never
         knowing my mother makes me love my
        children all the more.

Well, I sure am glad about that. …
Say, are you about done mixing that cake batter?

        Yes. Now go get your brothers and sisters so
        they can help you lick the bowl.

I was afraid you were going to say that.
Now, I won't even get a good taste.

Another Type of Bird

Mommy?

    Yes, Helen.

Mrs. Maggie Shannon offered me a
job at the Barnes Chief.

    Wonderful, Helen. But I thought you
    already delivered the papers?

No, Mommy. Maggie is going to teach me
how to set type. I'm going to help print the
Newspapers. Isn't that exciting?

    Yes, it is. What are you going
    to do with all of your money?

Well, Tommy and I are going to save some
money to buy a car. But first, I'm going to buy
some silky-underwear. I hate wearing those big
cotton-bloomers that everybody wears.

… Mommy?

    Yes, Helen.

Do you need any money for milk and food?

    No, Helen. But thank you.

I love you, Mommy.

    I love you too, Helen.

About Tommy—
On Soaring High

It was late and I couldn't sleep, so I went down to the dining room to rock in my chair.

I heard Tommy talking through the ceiling vents. She was telling Helen how she and her friends Bunny Black and Micky Holt climbed the water tower. Tommy said that she and Micky climbed to the very top and painted their initials by the light.

Well, I was about to go upstairs and give Tommy a good scolding, and perhaps a good smack on her hind end.

Then, I heard such a peaceful tone coming from her voice ... it caught me off guard.

Tommy declared, "Oh, Helen, what a wonderful feeling I had. It was beautiful up there... truly amazing... I felt as if I were half-way up to the sky ...I felt like I could almost reach out and touch a cloud. I wasn't even afraid of that rickety old ladder. I tilted my head up toward the sun and I felt the breeze on my face as it whispered past me. Oh, Helen, I will always remember what a complete sense of freedom I had ... the wonderful feeling of soaring high ... and almost flying ... just like a bird."

Well, after I heard Tommy say that, I couldn't very well punish her and take away such a beautiful, peaceful memory.

... some other time, perhaps.

Broken Wing

Levi was sharpening plow lathes
when he fell off an anvil.

He removed his shirt and noticed
his shoulder was deeply cut.

But Levi continued working.

At closing time, 6:00 p.m., Levi
locked up the Blacksmith shop
and went to the doctor.

The doctor merely sighed and shook
his head at Levi while applying ten
stitches to Levi's wound.

… That's my dad for you.

CAW

. . . .
Two sisters:
One sitting at the table, working on addition;
the other, working on making an addition to her pocketbook:
. . . .

        "Jean, I have already spent my money this
        week. Do you have any I could borrow?"

. . . .
Two sisters:
One voicing her handful of change;
the other, changing her tone of voice:
. . . .

        "I don't want nickels. I want dollars!"

. . . .
Two sisters:
One dumbfounded as the coins she handles, fly to the floor;
the other, flying off at the handle because of the coins:
. . . .

        "Just keep your money. It's not enough.
        I don't know what I'm supposed to do for
        fun, now."

. . . .
One sister:
Wanting more than anything to please her sibling.

One sister:
Never pleased with anything, always wanting more.
. . . .

The Clever Bird

Darlene is my oldest, and, my, what a clever little bird she is.

Darlene was a clerk at the local Safeway store in the neighboring town. During her lunch break, Darlene usually went across the street to eat at the A & P restaurant.

Darlene's boss often commented on how fabulous her work ethic was and how Darlene had a great way of communicating with the customers.

One afternoon, a young man entered the grocery store and politely inquired as to whether or not there was a public restroom.

Darlene blared out, "People at Safeway go over to the "A" and pee. But people at "A & P" say there is no Safe Way!"

The Bird with a Bill

Grandpa Bird?

    Yes, Donald.

Well …

    What is it, Donald?

Grandpa, sometimes I miss my dad when he's away working on the railroad… I miss him a lot.

    How old are you, now, Donald?

Eleven.

    Well, I'd give it another year and you can go with your father to work on the railroad yourself.

Really?!

    Yes, Donald.

Thank you, Grandpa Bird.

    You're welcome, Donald. (ha) I mean, 'Bill, Bill from over the hill, Never worked and never will.'

Goodnight, Grandpa.

    Goodnight, Donald.

Fly Away Little Birdie
Part II

Darlene? … Darlene?

        What, Virginia?

Do you believe in life after death?
I mean, do you really believe in Heaven?

        Yes, Virginia, there is a Heaven; it's
        called California and I'm leaving
        tomorrow to go there.

What? … Why?

        To write poetry and style hair.
        Do you want to go?

What did Mommy say?

        She said to follow my dream.
        You want to come with me?

Well …. Yes, of course.
I'd love to go …. with you.

High Pockets

Darlene Marie wrote soliloquies
And had a passion for poetry and verse.
Rhyming expressions,
Linked in succession
Excited her passion the most.
Nevertheless she had to
Express her love to the

Man she adored. Then …
Adding paper with pen,
Rhymes came again, and
Iambic
Expressions outpoured.

> All was beautiful.
> Darlene was a beautician,
> for women and for life.

Phil

Venus was the goddess of love,
Inclined to beguile her laughter.
Revolving with beauty (she was a cutie)
Gave way to much love ever after.
Instilled in Virginia — the same
Natural force,
Imparting her beauty to men (of course). She
Allotted her passion in elegant fashion, as

Love found exceptional force. But
Omissions came near,
Unwilling to hear; setting
Ironies strength to abound. So she
Struggled in vain and was left with her pain—as
Endeavoring tears—(((echoed))) sound.

> Virginia was a peacemaker;
> Pure of heart, and
> only wanting love.

Blue Jays

Sometimes Don was mean.
He often tortured Geraldine.

One day, for just a joke, he
made his little sister smoke;
… and he laughed at his attack.

Geraldine, against her will,
Smoked until she'd had her fill.

Then, absent all her charm,
she punched her brother in the arm;
… and cried when he hit her back.

Levi's Lament

Esther?

                Yes, Daddy.

Are you busy?

                What is it that you need?
                I can always make time.

Well … I was wondering if
you'd go to the cemetery with
me. Today is your mother's
birthday and I'd like to take
her some flowers.

                Of course I will, Daddy.
                Of course I will.

Mocking Birds

....

One of my neighbors had ten grandchildren; I will call their grandchildren, the 'Rich Bullies.' When the Rich Bullies were in town, they were usually mean to my children.

But my daughter, Tommy, was sick and tired of them. She was sick and tired of them all.
....

"Stop calling us names and
throwing rocks at us!"

> "What are you going to do about it, chase me down with those fancy sneakers you're wearing? Where'd you get those anyway; find 'em in a junk yard?"

"You're lucky my mother taught us to respect other people and other people's property."

> "Oh, yeah; well you're nothing but words."

....
Tommy was fuming, but she did what she felt she should do; she walked away. Tommy left and went to consult her friend, Bunny Black.
....

"I am fed up with those mean kids, Bunny.
What can we do?"

"Listen up, Tommy, I have a marvelous idea. Let's retaliate."

"How?"

"Well, I just happen to have two dozen ROTTEN eggs. You could practice your pitching skills."

....
Tommy grinned one of those sly-scheming smiles.
....

"Let's do it!"

....
Tommy hit the strike zone with every egg she threw that day.
....

....
Later, the 'mean' neighbor kids challenged Tommy and my other children to a game of 'Winner-Rule-All' softball.

My children quickly battered the egos of the rich bullies.

From then on, my children held their heads high, with no more disdain or judgment in social status from the 'rich bullies.'
....

....
'I am so very proud of my children.'
....

The Swan in a Uniform

Tippy-tippy-Tom, pitched the ball
— out threw them all.
Tippy-tippy-Tom, led the team
— was tall and lean.

She ran the bases,
Scored the points,
Won the games,
And iced her joints!

… But her game came to a halt—
and it seemed her dream would end
when she heard the news that day,
that would take her dearest friend.

        Tommy? Tommy?

What, Helen?

        Tommy, I'm going to California.

What? … How? … Why?

        I'm going to California. I'm taking a train.
        Virginia asked me to come out and help with
        her new baby.

What about school? What about our car?

        I'm going to go to school out there and
        probably ride around in one of those fancy
        San Francisco street cars. Good-bye,
        Tommy. See ya!

Good-bye, Helen… I guess.

Two Birds Flying in Circles

       Hey, Ken?

Yeah, Don?

       Did you see that great shot Gerald made
       at the basketball game today?

Of course I saw it. And I'll take
complete credit for it.

       What in the hell is that supposed to mean?

I'm the reason he's such a good player.

       No you're not.

Yes I am.

       No you're not.

Look. I made Gerald his first basketball goal at the Black Smith shop; I forge welded it. Ha! When I was making it, I'd look at it from the ground and thought it was just too damn big; so I made the hoop smaller. Then Gerald practiced on a hoop that was smaller than standard size and that's what makes him such a great player.

       He's a great player because he
       practices all the time.

He's a great player because of me.

       No he's not.

Yes he is.

       No he's not.

YES, he is.

Slow Poke

Her work ethic was the best in town,
Even after she left the Barnes Chief. When Helen
Left Kansas for sandy-beaches and healthy-ocean air, it
Enticed her desire for adventure. Helen
Never wanted to leave San Francisco. But

Money problems came to Virginia after a year or so,
And they were forced to leave the Golden State. —
Xeroxing her memories of California, Helen cried. She'd
Imagined herself living there forever and being happy.
Now, it was back to Kansas. — To Helen,
Everything seemed to be falling apart.

> Helen was in love
> with the beautiful
> landscape of California.

John

Knowing all that I had to endure,
Effectively brought Kenny and I very close.
Never did he allow me to over-work,
Never did he allow me to become sad.
Every stretch of time that his father was away,
Taught Kenny to be a better man, especially in the fields. I
Had noticed how many hours Kenny worked at the

Grocery story and the Wareham Hotel, so I
Excused him from all of his household chores.
Nevertheless, Kenny insisted on helping me. Kenny
Engraved my love in his heart. He is my true hero.

> Working hard in life
> taught my son to be valiant;
> and I was grateful.

Married to a Jail Bird

Virginia had married her prince of charm
And moved to the land of gold.
But her man gave warnings of alarm,
When confessions, to her, he told:

"Remember those gifts we gave to the folks?
Well, I stole them from the store.
At first, I did it for a joke;
But I have a job no more."

Virginia, of course, was mad and dismayed,
"What about the wagons, dolls and sleds;
All the toys with which my siblings played?
What about Mother's brand new bed?"

Her man, in regret, bowed with shame,
"I'm sorry, my darling; please forgive."
But Virginia decided to change her name,
And she found a new place to live.

About —
The 4th of July

Gerald?

      Yes, Mother.

My hands are covered with flour.
Could you please get in the top drawer
and hand me my rolling pin.

      Sure. What are you making?

Raisin pies and apple pies and rhubarb pies.

      I love raisin pies. What are they for?

The 4th of July picnic.

      We're having a picnic?

A picnic and a family reunion. Darlene and Virginia are
coming to visit and I get to see my new granddaughters.

      Good. I can't wait.

Neither can I, son.

      Mom?

Yes, Gerald.

      We should make that a tradition … the
      4th of July picnic and family reunion.

I think we will, Gerald.
I think we will.

I Love to Hear the Birds When they Sing

My children love to compete;
especially when they play cards.

They make everything a contest.

Well, okay, let's just say for
arguments sake that they
love to argue… always have.

They squawk and squawk
and squawk at each other.

Oh, my, how my children
love to compete.

Parakeets and Cockatiels
Playing Pinochle, Part I

Are you sure you can use a card
twice…on two different things?"

      I don't know what you're talking about.

If you have a run in Spades, you
can't use your queen with the
Jack of diamonds for a *Pinochle*.

      That's not using the queen twice; it's
      just making a *Pinochle* out of it.

Yeah, but will it still count for your
run? You can't have a run, plus a
Pinochle with the same Jack.

      I'm not using the Jack, I'm using the queen.
      You can use the same queen for a double-
      marriage and for a *Pinochle*. Even if I had two
      different *Pinochle's,* I could use the same queens
      and have two double marriages.

      Children, please. Stop your arguing.

      But we like to argue, Mommy.

Besides, we are not arguing, we are
professional debaters.

      Hey, that's my line.

No it's not. I said it first.

When the Score was Tied at Twenty

The score was tied at twenty,
Ken heard his brother say,
"When you deal the cards, don't be cheatin',
I know just how you play.
Oh, where's the Jack of Diamonds?
This pressure I cannot stand.
Come, dear brother, heed my words,
I need the Ace to win this hand."

The score was tied at twenty,
the tension rising high;
Ken took the deck of cards, gave
one to Don and kept one nigh.
Ken glanced across the table and
looked at Don who did not see,
when he cheated as he dealt the cards,
and gave the Ace to me.

Parakeets and Cockatiels
Playing Pinochle, Part II

Stop your cheating.

> Who's cheating?

Gerald. He's coughing to signal his partner.

> I'm not cheating. I just had to cough.

> A man has to cough, you know.

Stay out of it, Ken. — How do you like living in Colorado, Darlene?

> Now look who's cheating. Does Colorado mean clubs?

Ken, I said knock it off.

> Knock what off?

> Your beer. It stinks.

Yeah, why do you have to drink that?
It smells awful.

> I have to. It's a signal to my partner.

Leaving the Nest

Mommy, I'm going to Junction City to live with Virginia.

> What about school, Mary Ann?

I can go to school there.

> Well, if that's what you feel you need to do.

~

> Ann Mary...?

What, Grandpa, Bird?

> I don't know, Ann-Mary, are you sure you're fearless enough to live in a big city?

Yes, Grandpa.

> But you're only fourteen.

So.

> Ann Mary? ...

Bye, Mommy. Good-bye Grandpa Bird.
I Love you!

~

> Esther?

Yes, Daddy?

> What's happening with all of the children?

They are growing up, Daddy.

Night Owl

My bedroom window looked out onto
the front porch.
Late at night my curtains would be closed,
but I would lie in bed and listen for my
son to return home from work or from
being out with friends.

When I heard Ken's car pull up, or if I
heard his boots walking on the front porch,
I would reach up and pull a special string.
This string turned on the outside light.

After Ken was safely inside the house and
I heard his footsteps head toward his
room, I would reach up, pull the string,
and turn off the light.

I Know You're Talking, but all I Hear is Chirp, Chirp, Chirp, Chirp

Mary Ann called home to make an announcement.

"Mommy, I'm getting married."

The news displeased Ken.

"Mommy, she's too young to get married. I'm driving to Junction City and I'm going to talk some sense into her."

Ken hopped in his car and went to get his younger sister. Mary Ann, however, was stubborn and wouldn't listen to one word her brother said.

"You're too young to get married!"

"No I'm not!"

"Yes, you are!"

"No, I'm not!"

"Yes, you are!"

....
Ken put Mary Ann into his car and commenced on a very long drive back home. His intent was to lecture Mary Ann until she agreed with him, but they argued the entire trip
....

"You are way too young to get married!"

"No I'm not!"

"Yes, you are!"

"No, I'm not!"

"Yes, you are!"

....
As soon as Ken and Mary Ann arrived back home in Barnes, Kansas, Mary Ann left the house, went directly to the bus station and got on a bus headed for Junction City.
....

....
And yes, Mary Ann got married at the age of fifteen.
....

Gerald meets a Cardinal and Becomes a Sea Gull

You pronounce the name of my son, Gerald, with a Ga, sound, Not a Ja, sound. It's Guh, Gerald.

He won a contest from the grocery store which allowed him to travel to St. Louis.

Gerald attended a major-league baseball game between the St. Louis Cardinals and the Cincinnati Reds. He went to the St. Louis Zoo and visited the Lindbergh Memorial. He also took a one-day cruise down the Mississippi River on the S.S. Admiral.

He said his favorite part of the trip was riding on the S.S. Admiral.

He said, "Mommy, I want to be a sailor when I grow up. I want to sail atop the ocean. I want to travel the world and bring home many tremendous experiences."

… And that is exactly what he did.

Plumage

Darlene passed her worn trousers to Virginia,
who passed her mended sweaters to Helen.
Helen's work-boots were passed to Ken, and
Ken's winter coats … to Mary Ann.

Tommy's sneakers were all worn out;
So Don was passed over.
Tommy's dresses—not worn at all—
were passed to Gerry.

And last, but not least …all, except Gerald's Navy
uniform, were passed to Jean.
…All the faded flannels, some missing sleeves.
…All the shorts with broken zippers,
…All the trousers, patched and patched again.
…All of the half-pairs of shoes.
… All of the stitching, save nine.

But the clothes were more than just clothes to Jean.
… a story accompanied each and every garment.

… the trousers passed knowledge from
all the jobs of all the siblings.
… the cloaks passed all the lessons from
all the mistakes of the older nine.

Nine mentors,
…passing experience
…passing advice
…passing the way to walk the path of life.
…passing to Jean… competence… and

A bright and beautiful feather in her cap.

Love Birds

....
Darlene played cupid after Helen's return from San Francisco
....

              "Helen, this is Bob. Bob, Helen."

....
Ken played conniver to Darlene's playing cupid after Helen's return from San Francisco
....

   "Helen, Bob wants to take you to the 4th of July dance in Wabaunsee; you can ride over with me and Darlene."

....
Mary Ann confessed the truth about Ken playing conniver to Darlene playing cupid after Helen's return from San Francisco
....

      "By the way, Helen — Bob doesn't know you're coming."

           "What?! (gulp) Why would you do this to me, Kenneth? Turn this car around and take me home right now. Darlene what's going on?"

....
Bob was kind of mean after Mary Ann confessed the truth about Ken playing conniver to Darlene's playing Cupid after Helen's return from San Francisco
....

              "Hey! What in the hell are you doing here all dressed up?"

....
Helen was frenzied after Bob was mean when Mary Ann
confessed the truth about Ken playing conniver to Darlene's
playing cupid after Helen's return from San Francisco
....

       "How could you do this to me, Kenneth?
       How could you?"

              "Forget about it, Helen, just
              stay; enjoy yourself and have fun."

....
But all was well after Helen frenzied to Bob's being mean
when Mary Ann confessed the truth about Ken playing conniver to
Darlene's playing Cupid after Helen's return from San Francisco
....

              "Helen, would you like to
              Dance?"

    "I guess so."

....
After Helen's return from San Francisco she went to a party in
Wabaunsee and danced with a boy named Bob who was a friend of
Ken's that connived his sister into playing Cupid

Mary Ann swears it's the truth
....

Ann Mary
The Blue-eyed Stork

Married for five years, Mary Ann was twenty,
And pregnant with her first child. When she was
Ready to deliver, no one was around. She
Yearned for her husband. Mary Ann faced

Another hour of pain as she
Neared the moment of motherhood;
Never again would life be the same.

alas, it was time to give birth. With
nothing but her own two hands, Mary Ann
delivered her child. She smiled. She cried.

Born — was a precious son.
All was well with mother and child;
Baby slept in mother's arms.
Yes, all was well with mother and child.

> Her husband came home,
> in awe and proud of his wife
> for all she had done.

TOMMY

Love of playing baseball was
Overrated and visions of happiness were
Reduced to modest dreams. Tommy
Ran away from family to fight
Against her destitution; the move
Instilled determination from within. She had the
Necessary strength to
Embrace new accomplishments. However,

Financial prosperity was soon considered immaterial.
Remembering roots and family love became
As important to her as life itself.
Nature has an odd way of exposing character;
Circumstances follow the same path. Tommy learned that
Everlasting happiness will reveal itself in due course…
Such is life — with a heavy sigh.

> Remembering home
> and the love it provided,
> made her life complete.

About Darlene —
Moving to Colorado

Several years ago Darlene was expecting and
married, Bob; something she had not expected.

She expected Bob to be a good husband,
but the army transferred him to Japan, and
life got a little crazy.

When she delivered their third daughter, she found
out that Bob was crazy about a lot of other women;
she started to feel a little crazy herself.

Sadness moved inside of her heart
and Darlene moved back home.

Well, I expected her to stay with her dreams of
being a beautician; and told her so. And Darlene
was crazy enough to move to Colorado and open
up her own salon.

We expected life to be difficult,
but a crazy thing happened…
Darlene met Fred at the salon.
They fell in love.
Fred was loyal
and
life was good.
They got married and moved into a nice house.

Fred loved Darlene's girls as his very own. And
life was unexpectedly wonderful for Darlene.
How crazy is that?

About Kenny —
Becoming a Kingbird

When he was just a tiny-little bird
with a wagon rolling beneath his wing,
he found it foolish and absurd
and wondered what something else could bring.

After winter, he grew and he thought, that
a bike could show him different things;
so tires and chains and wheels he sought,
to help him soar into the spring.

And then a Robin sung his name,
and — four wheels turned below his wing.
… his life, beyond, was no more the same
when he heard that blessed creature sing.

Together they had other tiny-birds—
Ken made them toys and a swing.
His joy was one hundred, plus one third,
and he felt as would a king.

Bill, Bill From over the Hill
Never Worked and Never Will

Donald loved playing the card game, Pinochle, and
On occasion he played Pitch with my father.
Nonetheless, Pinochle was a favorite. His sisters
Accused him of cheating, which
Left Donald bewildered. But he knew he was just
Darn good at Pinochle and left it at that.

Donald fell in love with Judy Clark.
Until her, he had been kind of lonely.
After they were married, Donald joined the
Navy for four years and went to Hawaii. He never
Expected life to be so wonderful.

> Donald was in love.
> He had two boys and a girl
> And remained happy.

The Sea Gull

Gaining strength from family wisdom,
Everything was falling into place. Gerald
Replaced his passion for basketball, but only
After he joined the Navy. It seemed
Like it was the right decision to make. Gerald
Discovered a whole new world at sea.

Life was good for him, and
Entering manhood was
Even better.

> Gerald loved the sea,
> and he loved his mother.
> … he always wrote home.

Birds of Paradise
Part I

Helen wanted to visit Darlene in Colorado;
She saved her money with determination and will.
Jean was in a singing group with Gerry.
Gerry met Larry and Jean met Bill.

Levi was still buying Hershey's chocolate;
He had certainly eaten enough to get his fill.
Wesley came home from the railroad;
and he said that he loved me, still.

Tommy was dating a boy from the baseball team.
He proposed to her, but instead of saying, 'I will,'
Tommy replied, "I can't; we need to break up,
because I'm in love with Phil.

No more the Baby Bird

Mommy?

        Yes, Jean.

You know Richard Zimmerman?

        Your boyfriend?

Yes… well … maybe … maybe not.

        Oh?

I met Bill and I really like him.
I think I may like both of them.
I'm not sure what to do.

        Who do you love? Who can
        you see yourself marrying and
        having children with?

Well … that would be Bill.

        Jean… I believe you have
        answered your own question.

Setting Wings to Soar

The townsfolk were Not surprised when my
Father, Levi Bird, (pushing 90 years old)
still got up every morning and went to
work at the Blacksmith Shop.

The townsfolk were Not surprised that my
father still loved to eat Hershey's chocolate
candy bars.

They were Not surprised when my father
was ninety-one, and after conquering a
bout of Pneumonia, said he was tired and
wanted to be buried next to his wife, Etta.

The folks of the town, however, were very
surprised to learn that my father had been
deaf most of his life --- You couldn't tell
it from his speech, nor could you tell it
from his actions. My father read lips and
paid close attention.

The folks of the town knew that my father
was a passionate worker and loved his
Blacksmith shop.

But most of all,

they knew that he loved
his grandchildren…
more than anything else
in the world.

> Levi Leonard Bird
> 1867 - 1958

About Virginia —

I remember the time when Virginia ran away from home and Helen followed her.

Helen was determined to help her sister, but Virginia was so angry. She kept screaming at Helen to leave her alone.

Finally, Virginia punched Helen so hard that Helen fell to the ground ... hard.

Helen got up and kept walking.

Virginia came to a realization at that moment— when Helen ignored her.

Helen was tormenting Virginia with her own argument; it was Helen's way to make Virginia agree.

Then, making light of their endeavor, Helen said, "Oh, Virginia, I'm so hungry; please let's go back."

Together, they turned around and came home.

Now, I think of that time...so long ago and far away.

I think of that time when Virginia says to her own children, 'Be nice to your sister, now. Go and play.'

A New Song

I received a letter from Gerald today.
He is singing in the Navy choir.

Ken has joined the National Guard.
He and his wife have two little girls.

Tommy has two boys;
they help me mow the yard
and do the trimming.
They are such a blessing to me.

Last week I received a cassette tape
from the grandkids.
They had all gotten together
to sing me "Happy Birthday."

I now understand
why Levi
was so attached
to his
grandchildren.

Flying South

Gerald was away in the Navy,
Darlene was in Colorado, and
Virginia had moved to North
Carolina.

The rest of my children had
relocated to Kansas City.
My children were now having
children of their own.

~

Wesley and I lived in Northern
Kansas where the gentle
Breezes blew and the
Soothing rains fell upon
the wheat and
the corn stalks
in the field.

Nevertheless…
we were not prepared
for the
intemperate force of
nature that was
storming
inside
the lives
of our very own
children.

Searching for Shelter

During the day of a
bright and
beautiful morning in
the autumn of the year
when the clouds were high,
the birds were
singing joyfully and
the sun was
shining bright –
heaven opened
up the skies and
poured out darkness and
rain upon the birds, causing them
to flee from the happy existence
of all that they knew and loved.

Bird on a Wire

Hello, Mommy?

          Yes, Hello; Virginia.
          How are you?

I've been better, Mommy.

          What's wrong, Virginia?

Mommy, I have breast cancer.
I am going to have a mastectomy.

          What?

Do you remember that lump in my
breast the doctor said he was just
going to watch?

          Yes.

Well, he told me today that
it was cancer.

          I see.

Mommy, a year ago he reassured
me that since I was only 28 years
old, that I was too young to have
Breast cancer.

          (sigh)

Mommy?

          Yes, Virginia.

I'm scared.

          I know, Virginia. I know.

William Orton

William Orton is not a name recognized by most.

William Orton did not know me.
William Orton did not know my children.

William Orton was merely the president of
Western Union Telegraph Company.
His name appeared just below said title of
each telegram by said company.

But I knew the name of William Orton;
I knew it very well.

I received a telegram from the Navy.

I read the name of William Orton,
       over
           and over
               and over
         again …
            … Every day.

WESTERN UNION
William Orton, President

INFORMATION REGARDING GERALD

STOP

DIAGNOSED OSTEOGENIC SARCOMA

STOP

AMPUTATION RIGHT LEG SCHEDULED TUESDAY

STOP

MEDICAL DISCHARGE FOLLOWING

STOP

Birds of Passage

When Gerald came home from the Navy
he announced, "Mommy, I'm going to be a
preacher."

His spirit was stronger than ever…
spite the fact that he had but one leg.

Gerald wrote many sermons.

The sermons were mostly
about basketball,
and the Navy,
but he correlated them to God.

Gerald's spirit was stronger than ever…

Birding

Most people
love Christmas.
I do too,
but my favorite holiday
Is the 4th of July.

It's a happy time.

It's the time
I get to see
all
of
my
children

and

all
of my
continuously
growing
number of
grandchildren.

Funny

Going to different states and traveling with her husband
Enlightened Gerry on the ways of big-city life.
Rural living was no longer an option, as, once
Again, her music provided Gerry with many opportunities.
Life was so
Different now.
It was becoming intense and more complicated for her.
Not that she minded having an active life, but
Everything had changed.

Jean and Tommy remained close to Gerry. At every given
Opportunity they would talk and reminisce…
Yet Gerry's youth seemed so very far away. — Then
Children of her own were born… — And life was becoming
Ever-so-complete for Gerry.

Gerry loved to sing
She traveled from town to town
and shared her music.

Little Bohemian Pig

Joyous was the smile of Jean Carol. — With
Every passing day, you knew her life was at peace.
All who knew Jean, knew of her kind spirit;
None left her side without witness.

Caring for her children became the greatest
Ambition of her life. Singing was important as well, it
Reminded her of home. — Jean also loved the great
Outdoors. She loved the peaceful mornings when she
Listened to the birds as they sang.

> Jean, my youngest,
> is such a joyful girl.
> I love her so much.

Not all Birds can Fly but all Birds Have Feathers

Throw me that basketball, Gerald.
You just made a technical foul.

    It was an incidental foul. Don't forget, I've just got one leg.

    Oh, there he goes again,
    playing the handicap card.

Ha! You're right about that, Ken.

    Okay, I'll show you … Ah … he takes the ball .. he shoots outside the key … ooohhh … it's a swish and a score. … the crowd goes wild. — How do you like them apples, guys?

    Great shot, Gerald.

You know, shots made above the key
should be worth more points.

    Good luck getting that one in the rule book … All right guys, time to get started. I'm going to give you a six point lead, and I'll bet I can still beat ya!

    Let's get him, Don!

You are on, Gerald. Let's go, Ken.

    (cough) … Wait … (cough) … give me just a second.

    Here we go again.

An Old Bird learns a New Trick

Esther?

        Yes, Wesley?

What are all these damn little kids doing running
around our house and who do they belong to?

        Wesley! They are our grandchildren.

How many do we have?

        Nearly thirty, and more on the way.

Thirty? How'd we get so many?

        Wesley, we had ten children of our own.
        And the simple average of three children
        per family would give us thirty
        grandchildren.

Oh. … Well, since I'm retired from the railroad and
am the Town Marshall, I get to drive the Fire Truck.
… Do you think the grandkids would like to go for a
ride on a bright-red fire engine?

        I think that's a wonderful idea.

Okay. Well, tell them to get their shoes on then.
Oh… uh… Esther?

        Yes, Wesley.

I'm sorry about all of the hardships we've had,
and the way I've been.

        I know you are, Wesley. I know you are.

When He was Four and Twenty

The summer grew hot
and I grew weary.
As Gerald grew weak,
the sun grew dreary.

Night and day and day and
night, I sat by his side.
We talked and smiled and
spoke of life,
but neither of us cried.

~

> Gerald, my youngest son,
> turned twenty-four on the
> 12th day of September.
> Five days later, he died.

About — Virginia's Missing Feathers

One breast gone
… and then two

… cobalt treatments

… no lymph glands
… no eyebrows
… no hair, anywhere

… no boyfriend because of the missing breasts

… frozen lungs because of the cobalt

… no ovaries, now

… Is she still a woman?

Birds of a Feather

A portable oxygen machine is what gave Virginia the capacity to breathe; and to blow out most of the candles on her birthday cake.

It was a very happy party, though, Virginia made sure of that. She wouldn't allow pity. "I've lived a good life," she said, "and I'm not upset over dying."

We watched Ken's daughter as she clutched to the back of her father's legs…taking each step in unison right behind him and hollering out, "Look Aunt Virginia, I'm practicing to walk the same way my daddy does."

That's when Virginia looked at me and smiled.

I knew exactly what she was thinking.

She was reassuring me
that when one life ends,
another begins.

About — the Words
Virginia Spoke to her Siblings

"Living life
does not always mean
great length…

Loving each other
is what gives us
our strength.

My life has been special
because of you;

and vain will be my death,
if our tears are few."

Four months after the death of my son, Gerald, Virginia took her last breath. She was thirty-four.

…. Virginia left behind five young children.

In the Stillness of the Midnight

Daddy?

> Yes, Tommy.

Are you okay?

> No. This damn cough is about to get the best of me.

Is there anything I can do?

> Yes. Keep an eye on your mother.

What's wrong with Mommy?

> She grieves.

Grieves? Daddy, I've never even seen her cry.

> Tommy, your mother does all of her crying in the middle of the night. Promise me you'll watch over her.

I promise, Daddy.

My husband, Wesley, died of cancer two years after Virginia and Gerald.

Published

Darlene? How are you?

        Well, Mommy, I have great news.

Oh?

        Yes. My poem About Daylight Savings
        Time and soap operas was published
        in the T.V. Guide here in Colorado.

That's wonderful. I'm so proud of you. …

        Mommy?

Yes, Darlene.

        I have other news?

What?

        I don't quite know how to tell you.

Bird Brain

Doctor?

> Yes, Darlene.

Please don't just watch the lump in my breast.
Please just take it out.

> Listen, Darlene. You are very, very young;
> you've got nothing to worry about.

But cancer runs in our family.

> Please, Darlene, put off your silly notions.
> Cancer is not hereditary. Besides, women
> your age do not die of breast cancer.

I'm begging you, doctor.
Please, just take out the lump.
Remove my breast.

> Listen. I am the doctor and you are the
> patient. We're going to do it my way.
> Give it one year and we'll see what happens.
> Remember, you are too young to have
> cancer.

Pretty Bird

Mommy?

        Yes, Darlene.

I miss all of my clients at
the beauty parlor.

        Well, Darlene, you know you
        can't be around all of those
        chemicals at the shop because
        of your cancer treatments.

I know. I just miss making
all of my girls feel pretty.

        You'll be back to work
        soon enough, Darlene.

That's what I'm counting
on, Mommy. That's what
I'm counting on.

About Darlene —
Leaving Colorado

Praying tonight,
to find the light,
of sunshine without shadow.
It's been as wrong,
as the day is long,
except for Colorado.

She's not grown old—
or so I'm told—
but on her life's a shadow;
no cure has been found
the world around;
not even in Colorado.

The cancer has strength,
and she's failing at length,
to rid a blackened shadow—
Then…
"My Child," said He,
"Please come to me,
and leave your Colorado.

Reach toward the Heavens
across the moon,
toward the valley without shadow.
Come child, home,"
our Lord replied.
And she left her Colorado.

DNA

It's a peculiar
sensation in
your existence
when you realize,
that if the cancer
had contained a
different
nuclear
arrangement,
your children
would not be

dead
now
and

… lifeless, forever.

Bird in a Box

Five years, four gone.

It was no longer a matter of if,
It was a matter of when…
… and who.

We were all so numb.

Tommy had battled cancer as
well, but it was in remission.
We all prayed it would stay there.

The Bird Cage

Ken?

        Yes, Mary Ann.

What is going on with our family?

        I don't know.

Shouldn't we do something?

        My wife seems to think
        we should try to find
        a doctor that specializes in cancer.

That's a start.

        I feel like I'm living
        on borrowed time, Mary.
        Every day I live, I feel as if
        I owe someone for it.

So do I, Ken.　But we've got
to do something.
We've got to do something
for the sake
of our children.

Parakeets and Cockatiels Playing Pinochle, Part III

Hey, Gerry?

>What, Ken?

Get me a beer, will ya?

>I'm not getting you a beer. Beer stinks.

Fine! Hey, Don?

>>No! Get your own damn beer. I've got to figure out my strategy for the game.

>You mean a way to cheat, and signal your partner.

>>I do not cheat at cards. Grandpa Bird taught me that.

Children! Please!

Sorry, Mommy. ... Okay I'll bid... (cough)... eighteen.

>>You always bid eighteen... and cough when you have clubs. Stop your cheating.

I am not cheating!

>*CHILDREN !!!!*

A Little Bird Once Told Me

I thought about my father
and how he had coped
with the loss of his wife;
and how his loss
had given him a
true appreciation for life.

Levi had taught me
to be
emotionally strong.

… And for that
I will eternally
be grateful.

Without Words, Part I

If a tree in the
forest
falls
and no one hears,
does the bird
make a
sound
as she flies
away?

Without Words, Part II

Christmas came
and Christmas went,
no one talked about "IT."

Week after week,
month after month,
silence was the sound.

~

... She never said
a single word
to anyone.

... Each morning
she applied
a clean dressing
to her breast.

... Each evening
she changed
the blood-stained
bandages
because

... "IT" had eaten
through
her skin.

Without Words, Part III

Once again,
I watched in
sadness

as the mortician
closed the lid

on the coffin

to one of
my children.

Certain that the future of her young children would be
difficult, a mother is heartbroken as she takes her last
breath.

A ten year old little girl stands at her mother's casket.
She is unsure of life at this moment. She wonders
what her mommy feels like now. She reaches in
to touch the body.

Never will it be the same again. Five gentlemen sit in
bewilderment under the funeral tent. A man with
no wife; three teen-age boys without a mother; a father
who will never again see his daughter.

Cemetery sun; it shines with a blinding light; a blinding
light that forbids anyone to know tomorrow.

Every brother and every sister had wondered, "Will I be
the next to go?" "Why, at this particular time, was it
her instead of me?"

Remembering how important life really was, made them
truly appreciate what little time they had to share…
….what great love they had to give.

A Whisper of the Wind

During the lovely sun-lit moment of a bright and beautiful morning in the latter part of the month of April, a gentle, spring-breeze whistled softly through the bedroom window. The breeze revealed the imminent truth as it blew a delicate-silk blouse from the top of a stack of clothing—to the center of the bedroom floor.

I reached down to retrieve my daughter's blouse and after carefully folding it, I placed it into an open box on the Victorian-style nightstand.

I walked to the closet and gathered the slacks which were hanging on a pole, stretched across the width of the interior. I removed the slacks from the clothes-hangers and continued about my business.

After one last glance into the empty closet, I was briefly reminded of the many times Jean had frantically searched for something to wear. I closed the door and sighed. When I turned, I was invited back to the necessary task set before me.

When the very last article of clothing had been boxed-up, I walked to the window and without faltering I closed the pane and pulled the shade, which disconnected both the breeze and the light that had once found its way into the room.

I carried the boxes downstairs and stacked them on the back porch. I carefully wrote across each box, "Salvation Army." And then, as if my most recent undertaking had been part of my normal-daily routine, I walked into the kitchen and asked my grandchildren what they wanted to eat for dinner.

About — How I Reacted on that Particular Day

Ken's wife had witnessed all that I had witnessed. …
Don's wife too. …. My daughters … my sons …
I listened as they spoke.

~

How could Jean do this to us, Tommy?   Never
saying a word to anyone about having cancer.

> I'm sure Jean had her reasons.

Like what?

>> Like not wanting Mommy to fret night and day
>> and day and night because another one of her
>> children was dying.
>> Like not wanting everyone to feel sorry for her
>> because she had no insurance … no way to pay
>> for cancer treatments.

Oh, so she just up and decides not to let us help her. That's
not being fair to us. Esther would have given every last
dime she had to help Jean pay her medical bills.

>> Jean didn't want Mommy to lose her house!
>> Jean knew that Mommy would mortgage
>> everything to pay the doctor bills.

>>> Girls! Please don't argue.
>>> This is my fault.

Mommy! This is not your fault.
Why would you say such a thing?

>>> "I have bad blood."

"What!"

"I have bad blood and
bad cells and I've
passed them to my
children."

"Stop talking nonsense."

"No. It's true. It's all
my fault."

"Mother! It is not your fault. It's no one's fault.
Look at Daddy's side of the family, the same thing
has happened to them …His brother lost six out
of six….his sister three out of five, all to cancer!
It was on his side, too; that's why it's been so
dominate with us.

But my mother died
young of breast cancer.
Two of her sisters died
young of breast cancer.
It's my fault they were
all so young.

Mommy, don't. That's still no excuse for Jean.
She should have told us.

STOP! Jean didn't tell anyone …
because of me.

What? What do you mean by that, Tommy?

She didn't tell anyone because she
knew that my cancer was back.

PLEASE, GOD .. NO
… PLEASE…DON'T!
NO… I CAN'T!

A Tough Old Bird

A few weeks later, I could see that
Tommy's cancer had come back.

But she acted as happy as a lark,
like nothing was wrong … like
life was normal.

There she was … my little Tommy,
pretending life was a baseball game
with two out and the bases loaded.

About — The 1977 4th of July Reunion

I overheard one of my granddaughters
talking about all of the things she
wanted to accomplish in her life
before "IT"
happened to her.

I couldn't believe my ears.
She was accepting
our family situation
as a normal circumstance.

There are
no words
to explain
how I feel.

… None.

As the Wind Blows

"Kenny! Don! I am so glad to see you!"

"Tommy?"

"Yes, Kenny."

"Why are you so happy?
Don't you know why they called us all in."

"Oh, you don't understand. Everything is ready and I've even got a pink cross for my grave. — I get to go home. — Darlene & Virginia, and Jean & Gerald, and Grandpa, and even Daddy are waiting for me."

"You can see them?"

"Yes. Yes, I can. — I want you to know that I love you all so much and want to thank you for giving me such a wonderful childhood.

"Wonderful? Don't you remember how poor we were?"

"Don't you remember how much fun we had together…laughing and arguing and being competitive? I wouldn't trade it for the world. Not for anything."

"Tommy?"

"Yes, Don."

"We love you, too."

Tommy died the next day.

About — My Thirteen Year-old Granddaughter

She scolded her little brother for smelling bad.
She yelled at him to take a bath and wash his hair.
The next morning, her brother was clean, but she was angry to suddenly be responsible for his hygiene.

She was coming into womanhood. She left a note on her father's nightstand that said, "Dad, I need some Kotex."
The next morning, instead of Kotex, there was a twenty-dollar bill on her father's nightstand. She felt embarrassed as she waited in line at the grocery store.

She sat in front of her mother's tombstone at the cemetery. She told her mother how much she missed her and needed her.
The next morning, her mother was still dead.
She knew she would have to grow up, take care of her brothers and not take life so seriously.

She came to see me. "Grandma," she said, "I don't understand all of these things." I tried to be of comfort. "Grandma," she asked me, "can I please have that picture of my mother?"
The next morning, she left to go back home, and she was happy.

Mary Ann and Me

It was Mary, who many a year ago
that talked about the 'C'.
And she talked about others, whom you may know,
that lost their loved ones, like me.
And Mary she lived with no other thought
then to find a cure for the 'C'.

I was her mother and she was my child;
we were as happy as could be,
But we shed our tears and shared our fears,
When she told me about her 'C'.
I then prayed out to the God up in Heaven
to save her from the 'C'.

But God has his reason for saying no,
witnessed by Mary and me.
A storm came down on her life by day,
as she fought against the 'C',
and she lost her battle when the good Lord came
and took her away from me.
We placed her inside of a coffin
And we buried her with her 'C'.

I was not happy with God up in Heaven
and he was not happy with me,
But I had my reasons as all men know
For raging against God and 'C',
— For He took the ones who were not willing;
He took them away from me.

… But God's love is stronger by far, than those
who cannot comprehend,
than those who do not understand.
And none of the angels in heaven above
nor Mary who drowned in the 'C',
could ever divide my soul from the God
Who has loved me … in spite of me.

Now in my dreams, I see Mary it seems;
her soul is happy and free.
I've opened my eyes to the God who is wise;
who has loved me in spite of … me.
I know Mary is home, in her spirit I see
her love that was given to me.
—And now she will live, in spite of the 'C',
—She will live through the love inside me.

About — The Birthday Party

I went to one of those fancy-city-restaurants to have a pretend birthday party for those of my children who have passed on.

I decided to make September the month in which to celebrate, since four of my children were born in September and two of them died in September.

When I walked into the restaurant I knew it was an appropriate place for the party; but when I saw how crowded the dining area was, I asked the waitress if I could be seated outside on the patio. I was already feeling a lump in my throat and knew my eyes could begin watering at any moment. I didn't want the other patrons to feel sorry for me.

I was seated outside. It was a beautiful day.

The waitress started to give me a menu but I held up my hand and declined the offer. I explained to her why I was there. I asked for a piece of carrot cake, two scoops of ice cream and six candles; one candle for each of my children in heaven.

The waitress stared at me with wide eyes and said, "You're going to make me cry," at which point I almost did as well.

She left to fill my order and I listened to the music playing on the speakers. I knew my children would never allow me to bring them to such a fancy place, but too bad, if they were here, this is where I would bring them.

The waitress returned to my table with the cake and ice cream. She set the plate on the table, lit the candles, and looked at me, once again, with those big Bambi-eyes. She then touched me on the shoulder and left me alone to have my party. I examined the cake and noticed it was big enough to serve ten.

I began singing "Happy Birthday" inside of my head. Just then, an unexpected breeze flittered by and blew out two of the candles. I began to cry; it wasn't fair for those flames to be quenched before their time. — It was at that point I thought the party would be an emotional disaster. However, I wiped my tears, picked up my fork and proceeded to take a bite of ice cream; but the caramel from the ice cream was drizzling down and I had to twirl my fork to keep from making a mess. It reminded me of the way Gerald used to eat spaghetti. — I laughed out loud.

I then remembered how Tommy used to blend her ice cream with her cake; she would say, "I like 'smushing' it together, it tastes better." So that's exactly what I did ... I 'smushed' some of it together.

The more I thought about my children, like the way Mary Ann used to complain about not getting enough of the raw batter when I made cakes, and the way Darlene carried Jean around on Jean's first birthday, and how Virginia asked me to bake a fancy carrot-cake for her birthday instead of the usual chocolate ... I smiled.

I realized birthday's are for celebrating one's life. So that is exactly what I did that day. — I had a fine celebration and it was fun.

It was a beautiful day.

About — Time

As trees grow
… birds sing
… flowers bloom
… love arrives
   and
   time endures.

As time endures
… colors fade
… leaves fall
… love is remembered
   and
   birds fly away.

I had eleven children.
Only four outlived me.

~

Esther Mina Bird
1904 - 1981

Birds of Paradise
Part II

In heaven I saw my mother, Etta. She was waiting for me to come home.

We embraced.

She told me what a brave woman
I had been on earth.

She said, "You are a valiant soul."

I learned a lot about life after I died.

… As all do.

The Flight Continues
Parts I, II, III, IV & V

When Ken's daughter was younger,
she walked in his shoes.

Now that Ken was older,
he was beginning walk in my shoes.

His daughter was diagnosed with breast cancer.
She was twenty-eight years old.

The family screamed out, "ENOUGH IS ENOUGH!"

They finally found someone who would listen.
They joined a medical research study.

Ken's daughter died anyway ... she lived to be thirty-four.

A second daughter followed. – Surgeries – struggles –
— staying strong - smiling - screaming out –
"What have I done?" "Please don't take me away from
my children." — Succumbing to an unwanted death.

~

One of Virginia's — The same as above.

Two of Darlene's were diagnosed as well
— but one actually survived.

She was the only one in our family
to survive cancer.

— The only one. —

The Flight Continues
Part VI

The family's curse
of cancer
went on…

Diagnosed, very young,
age twenty-seven;
Don lost
his only daughter.

But to say 'lost,'
is an unspeakable
misrepresentation
of words.

Don had watched
his baby girl
as she fought
… and fought
… and fought
… for her life.

But to say 'fought,'
would be a
horrendous
understatement
of combat.

Posthumous Fame

… Famous?

… In a medical journal.

… they were part of a
study that led researchers to
find the hereditary cancer gene.

… They would rather have
known their children.

… They would rather their
children have known them.

Let's Put 'it' to Rest

Cancer – When I think of it now, I think of "Black." I think of a bubbling, ..~..~.. scalding substance that diminishes and ~.~.~.~. deteriorates everything in its path. It is relentless and persistent. It moves slowly and slashes deep into your emotions. It adheres itself to your mind and nothing, absolutely nothing in the world, will let it be released from your thoughts.

~

I have witnessed a failing fight against this disease. But thank goodness times have changed. Research and technology has improved and we need to support that research, educate ourselves, and keep moving forward.

We need to constantly be aware. We need to avidly support the fight for the cure.

Air Above Wings

It's been almost thirty years
since I've come
to heaven.

I am allowed
to look down
upon the earth …

I see Ken & Don
and
Helen & Gerry
who are still alive.

They have kept watch over
my precious grandchildren.
…my grandchildren without
mothers.

They still gather at those
4th of July reunions
I started so many years ago.

It is the one place we all
find each other.

… for now.

About the Author

Rebecca Stallard earned a Bachelor's Degree in English and Communications at Missouri Western State University. She collaborated with her colleagues from Missouri Western to create a historical film about the History of St. Joseph, Missouri, entitled, *To Cross a River*. Rebecca worked as line producer, dialogue editor and scene revision editor. She has worked as a screenwriter with Margaret & Margaret Productions in Los Angeles, and has a self-published children's book, *Cari Fry in the Land of Nye*. Some of her other works have been entered into *Slamdance* and *Big Break* competitions.

Rebecca is a member of the Kansas City Chapter of the Missouri State Poetry Society. Her work from the organization can be found in *Kansas City Metropolitan Verse, Volumes I & II*. She currently directs the creative writing program at a high school in Kansas City, Missouri.

Rebecca was born and raised in Kansas City. While growing up, Rebecca often heard that she was living in a family cursed with genetic cancer, and that she and her family members should live life to the fullest while they were young.

When Rebecca was 13, she not only witnessed the death of her mother to breast cancer, but realized the family's 'supposed genetic-mutation' was a realistic truth. Nineteen of her first cousins had lost their mother to cancer and the disease was also entering into the lives of the next generation... her generation.

Rebecca set out on an intense path to accomplish her goals. She graduated as Salutatorian of her high school class, but set aside college to raise her children before the assured family-fate fell upon her own life. To offset the uncertainty of her future, Rebecca began to write poetry. Although it was an outlet, the ambiguity of her life haunted her thoughts.

In the mid 1980's, as yet another one of her cousins was enduring chemotherapy treatments for breast cancer, the family joined a medical research study. Her cousin died, but was probably one of the main links to the study. Several years later, researchers revealed the discovery of the hereditary breast cancer gene (BRCA1). Rebecca and members of her family were given individual results of the test. Rebecca was found negative to having the gene.

As a single mother, she then set out to achieve goals that, before now, had been set aside. In college she studied English and Theatre for the sole purpose of writing her family's story. Rebecca has written the story of her family, entitled, *Pinochle* in both screenplay and stage-play form. Rebecca has since returned to her love of poetry and has written her story in the poetic-verse narrative, *And the Birds are Singing*.

Rebecca also loves biking and tennis, but most of all, she considers herself very privileged to witness her children grow to adulthood.

Her mother ... was, Tommy.